FROM

THE

BEGINNING:

MEMOIRS

Mary Jo McKeon

From the beginning, I wasn't who I was supposed to be. Before my parents could take me home from the hospital, they had to register my name with the birth clerk. The plan was to name me after my great aunt, who was a Roman Catholic nun. "That's not a name" admonished the clerk "Mary Josina? Who ever heard of a name like that?" So my birth certificate reads: FIRST NAME: MARY JOSEPH. My baptismal certificate: MARY JOSINA.

Years later, when I was in 5th grade, I wanted my teacher to call me JOSINA, probably because I thought it was cool. "OK, dear, that's fine. Just tell me how to spell it." I had no idea.

Maybe I've been trying to be someone I'm not since I was born. Mary Joseph: who ever heard of a name like that?

But a name has meaning and it has power. It's your birth title. A name tells the world, it tells you, who you are.

»¨« »¨«

These are memoirs.
They are part of a saga
that can be divided roughly
into sections: Mary Jo -
the sick years #1; The
Phoenix Rises; Mary Jo -
the ABC News years begin;
The sick years #2 and the
Worm Starts to Turn;
Mary Jo seeks higher
education (because, after
all, she is Irish); Love;
Librarian to the stars;

More learning; Retirement;

Mary Jo keeps on writing.

σσσ

Birds on a wire, we three 9 year old girls sat in Lennon Park, watching a circle of boys play baseball. Our bench had cement sides that reminded me of ice cream sprinkles, the green paint on the wooden slats was peeling.

A rock hit us, but we thought it was a fly ball. My best friend was next to me and shouted in panic "Mary Jo, you're bleeding!" There was no pain – but the alarm in her voice sent me reeling and we ran to my house, four blocks away.

It was a Saturday and Dad was home. He thundered to the park and somehow brought a 10 year old boy to my house, demanding that he apologize. Dad was an intimidating, large man. The boy, in his short pants and sneakers, quaked and stammered, looked at the floor: "Sorry". Then Dad took me to the Emergency Room.

That could have been the start of all my future brain problems. But by the time the serious stuff surfaced, I didn't remember this sunny summer morning.

These early years are spotty. Before we got too friendly to continue our professional relationship, a psychiatrist once asked me to shut my eyes and speak of the images that appeared describing my childhood. After a

while, I said *there is a
little girl, maybe 2 or 3,
wearing a long white
nightdress with curly,
light colored hair,
dragging a stuffed
brown bear by the arm.
She walks to a huge oil
tank, round and green, a
staircase winding
around it with a
platform at the top.*

The girl climbs the stairs and peers over the edge into a black nothing.

"You must be terrified," the therapist says. "You know that girl is you, right? And you should be grateful that what she sees is a black nothing. That's your childhood. You don't need to see it. Living it was enough."

So I was told that my early years were awful, but that's not my memory of them. My first vivid mind image is me standing at the kitchen sink, watching my mother wash dishes. I think I want to help, not sure. Anyway, I'm too short.

^^^

My family didn't mingle with other relatives; they didn't mingle with anyone, really. I don't remember parties or gatherings. But I do recall a dinner with my grandmother, my mother's mother. She'd just returned from a trip to her homeland, Ireland. Afraid of shipboard theft, she'd left her wedding ring and Tiffany diamond engagement ring, small but classy, with my parents. The rings, sealed in a small manila envelope, were to be given back over coffee.

After the meal, we kids were sent up to bed. Although my sister doesn't have the same recollection of the way this night played out, my memory has me listening in the dark at the head of the stairs, trying to hear what the grownups were saying. But the heavy swinging door that separated the kitchen from the dining room muffled everything. Though I heard coffee cups and dessert plates being set on a tray in the kitchen, as soon as my mother let the door swing behind her,

sounds got faint.

The voices,

however, began to rise

in volume.

The exact

conversation has

become family

lore/hearsay but

suffice it to say that

Grandmother had no

use for my father. She

felt that mother had married beneath her; Dad was not directly from her family tree, and was therefore worthless. Bullheaded belief can be as deep - and dark - as the Atlantic Ocean.

We kids didn't think Daddy was

worthless. We'd jump up and down on his belly at night; I didn't know or care that it was a beer belly. He'd read SCUFFY THE TUGBOAT to me and wove tales from his head: like the ongoing story of the McGuillicudy Family and their trips to the P&A

grocery shop to buy
cans of Chock Full O'
Crocks coffee and
packages of Rag-A-
Muffin-Muffins. They
used "sKissors" and ate
"sWord fish: dad
purposely twisted
phrases and
mispronounced words to
our frustrated but
joyful squeals of

protest that he "was wrong".

Mother was plagued by something called a proteous organism that ravaged her body. She spent most of my younger years in and out of hospitals. This organism is a sneaky, nasty thing;

there were frequent attempts to catch and remove it.

But when I was in 4th grade and the underdog in a singing contest at some parochial school miles away, she was there cheering me on. Despite having just come home from one of her

exploratory hospital
trips, she was sitting on
rough gym bleachers,
undoubtedly sore and
very uncomfortable.
Determined love as
deep as the ocean.

ΘΘΘ

So why did a
therapist tell me to be
grateful my memory of

childhood is "black nothingness"? As I said, these memories are sporadic but weighing it all, adolescence sounds pretty good so far, right?

So far doesn't always linger long.

***

A whirl of white rushed over to my bed holding the longest needle I'd ever seen. My poor parents sat with me, helpless to ease their child's fright.

But I was blissfully unaware of the seriousness of my situation. All I knew

was dad brought weekly
shopping bags full of
Busy Baker chocolate
chip cookies. The
neighborhood bakery
adored my larger than
life father with the
wife who was always in
the hospital and now
one of his four kids
was, too. Everyone

loved Tom; it was the

least they could do.

The nurse in the

sharp white

uniform plunged

the needle into my

left thigh.

~~~

A call from

Montefiore Hospital

alerted my mother that a bed had become available. Her 6th grader (me) had been coming home for weeks with debilitating headaches. From the start, we McKeon kids were aware of the power of words; so when a 12 year old repeatedly says "I can't take this anymore", I knew my parents would listen. Mother even moved the furniture in my room, thinking that the older house was sinking, causing blood to rush to or away from my head.

When I kept coming home in tears, she took me to the

family doctor who had the good sense to know he didn't know what was wrong. Dr. Queally suggested my mother take me to The Headache Unit at Montefiore Hospital in the Bronx. That doctor examined me and told her (he didn't talk to me because I was a minor) that there was nothing wrong: "It's puberty", he said. "Her body is adjusting to changes within." But to be on the safe side, he'd run some tests in the hospital. "It's not an emergency", he said, "so you'll have to wait until a room opens."

One of the advantages of a large teaching hospital like Montefiore is that the patient has the benefit of visiting doctors. Often my parents and I would come face to face with ME on the chalkboard in the lounge: the medical symbol for female, the date 06/07/1953 and the word Caucasian. There were also some other words, unpronounceable and even unrecognizable to me like "cerebellar astrocytoma" and "Torkildsen Shunt". But my family and I thought this sight was a kind of badge of fame: my

name in lights, even
though the name was
not spelled out.

Even so, I had a
queasy feeling in my
stomach, like looking at
myself from under the
water: why were these
faceless people talking
about me?

Before CT scans came along in the 1970s, a medical test called a pneumoencephalogram was what the medical community had to look at brain function. This test started with a spinal tap and was unbelievably painful. The day after I had

the exam, the doctors
told me they had to do
it again "because the
film was foggy" and
they couldn't get a
clear reading. "You do it
again and I'll kill
myself", I told them.
My child's mind even
developed a course of
action: somehow I'd
break into the locked

room behind the nurse's station where sharp medical instruments were kept and I'd cut my wrists. An extremely flawed plan but scary that a 12 year old would even think about suicide.

Mom and dad recognized my resolve.

They agreed to the
more invasive but less
painful (because I
would be under
anesthesia) procedure
of full on brain surgery.
I need to say this again:
the anguish those two
young parents, my
parents, had to be
feeling is unimaginable.
They'd just agreed to

let their child have
brain surgery, even
though they had no way
of knowing if it was
necessary. Concern as
deep as the ocean plus
a recognition that this
child was no longer 12,
but far more worldly
wise.

They believed I'd
have found a way to

fulfill my plan, however
flawed. I was cut from
their genes.

%%%

As the gurney
wheeled me to the
elevator with those
buffer blankets on the
walls and descended to
the freezing OR, the
"needle nurse"
whispered that I'd

start to feel groggy and soon would be asleep.

My eyelids were heavily closed but it was very bright and there was a smell, like burning leaves, and a sound, like the dentist office. I shouted (though it probably came out as a mumble) to my friend Judy to "get out of here –

there's danger here".

The OR nurse yelled

"Oh my God, this child

is not yet under!" (Her

shout wasn't mumbled,

it was loud and clear

and full of alarm.) Of

course, I was

hallucinating but the

pain nerves were

mercifully blocked. But

I could hear and I could smell. To this day, I'm a basket case in the dentist chair.

During the procedure, the surgeons saw a growth and snipped off a piece for the lab to tell them if it was cancerous. It was not. The term benign can mean "no problem". But not always. The mass sitting at the base of my brain prevented the flow of liquid from one side to the other. Pressure built up and that was the cause of my horrendous headaches.

But because of the location, removing it

would be tricky. Not
wanting the risk of
paralyzing the child on
the table, they decided
to leave the tumor
there and insert a
newly invented shunt, a
type of valve or bridge,
that would allow fluid
to flow through it,
bypassing the growth.

It worked for 16 years
and then the shunt fell.

≈≈≈

    If there was
anything not awful
about my illness, it was
timing. And they say
that timing is
everything. By
September, I was back
in 7th grade. There
were few external

reminders that
anything had happened.
Except for the horrible
yellow wig that I wore
every day.

Here's that story:

As I recovered in
my private room, the
hospital staff
recommended that
since there would be a

summer of radiation treatments, I should have a wig for my fall return to school. My father, who always seemed to find the unfindable, befriended a wonderful middle-aged couple who ran a hair salon in the Bronx, not far from the hospital. They actually came to my bedside

with samples

of hair pieces. Sitting

in a beautiful brocade

case with a zipper

around the middle, a

brassy blond hooker wig

sat on a Styrofoam

head. That's the one I

chose and no one had

the heart to talk me

out of it. At the start

of the new semester, I
wore a horrible mop on
my bald head. But I
thought it looked great.

A month later, I
was home and obsessed
with the hair that had
been cut off. My
mother had saved it and
she tried to prevent me
from seeing it for as

long as she could, but I
badgered her every
day. When she opened
the bag it was in, I
cried. It was not at all
what I "remembered":
beautiful, curly blond
hair, soft and shiny.
The hair in that plastic
bag was a tangled,
mousey brown mess. In
my eyes, the yellow wig

grew more stunning every minute.

~~~

Even in Catholic school, recess ends all too soon. The shrill bell signaled that we should file inside and line up. Girls were on one side, boys the other: we'd been trained to separate ourselves by

grade. Suddenly, one of
the boys broke rank,
ran over to me, and
yanked my wig. It flew
to the floor before me.

I had one of those
moments when my brain
didn't know what signal
to send out, so my body
took over. Moving
forward, I picked up
the yellow mass,

continued straight into
the principal's office
and, safe within that
sanctuary, sobbed like I
hope never to sob again.
The nun who sat there
rose and walked over to
me, actually put her
gnarled hand on my
shoulder, and said
"You've had a terrible
shock. I could call your

mother to come take

you home. But my

advice to you is to

march to your

classroom with the

other boys and girls as

soon as you collect

yourself. The longer

you wait to go back, the

more difficult it will be.

Of course, it's your

choice. But if you are

going to go, do it now and walk into class before everyone has taken their seats." That's what I did. I was 13 now and could appreciate the wisdom of her words.

But when I came home, my mother was: how to even say it?

Confused, angry, sympathetic, outraged? And when dad got home from work, he was wild with his own mixture of super-charged emotions. He demanded to know who the culprit was and, shades of a little boy standing in my house years earlier after throwing rocks at

three 9 year old girls,
he brought this new boy
with his father to our
house. This time,
though, if there was an
apology, I didn't hear it.
I couldn't or wouldn't
leave my bedroom.

~~~

One more episode
from elementary
school, not as gut

wrenching but terrible in its own way.

The pastor of the parish was coming to my 8th grade class in anticipation of the Catholic rite of Confirmation. The nuns were atwitter with excitement and I suppose so were we children.

The great man and my father worked together in a church capacity, but unknown to me, they hated each other: two blustery big Irish peacocks who didn't like taking instructions from anyone but craved the limelight, unaccompanied.

The priest asked the class, "What happens when you die?" A few of us had the nerve to raise fluttering hands. Deeply bellowing "Miss McKeon", he pointed to me. Proudly, I stood and said "When you die, you see God." He roared again "You ignorant, silly girl!! How can you see anything when you have worms in your eyes?" The nuns shook in the presence of blasphemy. I trembled before a bully who reminded me in so many ways of my father.

On to high school.

The Catholic Church built my high school. The impressive looking round granite building housed a segregated group of students: girls in one wing, boys in the other. The only time the sexes came together was for religion class once a week and we felt safe in this space. The teacher, a Christian brother, was young, "hip" and encouraged us to let our hair down and speak freely.

One day Brother Tom wanted to talk about something called "transubstantiation" - that part of the Mass when the bread and wine turns into the body and blood of Jesus Christ. "This is a basic principle of the Catholic church", he said. A sincerely religious student spoke of the empowerment she experienced when the priest raised the host and the wine and they "become" the body and blood of Christ.

"Penny", I said, "your

faith is beautiful and

must bring you so much

comfort. I truly envy

you but I just can't

believe this really

happens."

Shortly after these

religion classes, Penny

was diagnosed with

brain cancer. She lived

a block down the street and phoned early one morning. She asked that I come by to tell her if she looked OK without her wig. "You're the only other person I know who had to make this decision", she said. I did go and she looked fine. Unfortunately, Penny Ward died a year later. It's impossible to understand why bad things happen to good people, but this girl's pure faith touched a lot of other lives. Maybe her mission had been fulfilled.

***

In my junior year, I was summoned to the principal's office and introduced to a man from The Office of Vocational Rehabilitation. This government department existed to financially aid a disabled person's educational re-training.

"You were in a car accident, I see from your records", he said.

"What?" I replied.

"Well you had brain surgery..." he trailed off. "Yes", I said, "But it wasn't the result of a car accident." "Well no matter the cause, we will pay for your college, anywhere in the country, including room & board and books, because we feel that your early surgery put you at a disadvantage. You are entitled to be taught a new skill." Though this may be part of my own lore, the response "I did want to be a gym teacher" sits in my memory bank. It was probably just a thought, though.

I have no idea who
arranged the offer.
Maybe it was my
guidance counselor,
maybe it was outreach
by this mysterious
government office, but
it turned out not to be
completely true. I
wound up attending a
New York State college
and though my tuition

was paid, the room,
board and the books
were not. Still, an
unexpected gift from
an unlikely source.

≥≥≤

With my father's
gift of the Blarney
Stone, people were
drawn to me. But I
always felt like I was

standing outside the scene, like a fly on the wall. Kids called me to help them with homework, but not to come out drinking with them. My truly close friends were few in number: I could count them on one hand. Maybe many high school kids feel this way.

However, by senior class, I was not only president of The National Honor Society, but president of my (girls) class. So where did my sense of inadequacy and low low low self esteem come from? And more important, why is it still with me?

How do I change this
self-perception?

≤≤≤

When my mother
was in Cabrini High
School in the Bronx in
the 1930s, ballroom
dances were not only
the rage, they were the
norm. She had fabulous
clothes: a long black
velvet gown with miles

of material in the skirt

a matching evening

cape, also black velvet,

with an ermine lined

attached hood. She

loved beautiful things,

and always found a way

to pay for them. Her

father had died when

she was young, 8 or 9,

and her mother

somehow bought and

ran a boarding house.
There was no real
money, just loads of
determination.

I inherited that
resolve and it's both a
good thing and a curse.
In the blessing
category, I wanted to
wear that dress in a
school play, singing
Birth of the Blues. I

had to lose at least 10 pounds in 3 weeks. Placing a calendar on my bedroom wall, I ticked off each day and wrote down my weight. It worked and the mental image is still fresh in my mind's eye.

Shortly before high school, I switched from my awful yellow wig to a light brown hair piece called a fall. It matched my existing hair color and reached the middle of my back. The new hair was attached by a black velvet head band. My radiation treatments were cobalt, which kills

hair follicles; no amount

of Rogaine would ever

bring back the hair on

the back of my head.

The day I went

with my mother to the

hairdresser was an

emotional one, and she

took me shopping to

lessen the distress.

She found a fine blue

wool cape, almost floor
length, with a silver
lion's head clasp at the
throat. It cost a
fortune but I felt like a
million bucks wearing it.
"You must have that",
she said. Weakly
(because I didn't want
to talk her out of
buying it), I asked "But

the price - what will Dad say?"

We walked to the car and in a few minutes, she answered "This is how we handle things. When we get home, you give your father a fashion show. He will be so delighted to see the glow on your face, he won't even ask how much the cape

cost."

The lessons I

learned that day were

these: first: my own

reaction might control

the outcome. Next: if

you want something

desperately, figure out

how to jump all hurdles

between you and it.

Lower your head and

charge. Twirling before him, Daddy was in the palm of my hand forever. He might have been a blustery bully, but he didn't stand a chance.

~~~

College (SUNY Brockport)

Never took a math class and I never took a

science class. This is
not something I'm
proud of but it says
something about who I
am: determined NOT to
take on things unless
fairly confident I'll
succeed. So, I took
every *ORAL
INTERPRETATION OF
LITERATURE* class
available. These were

both easy and fun but I was perhaps the only student who loved getting up in front of the class to speak. My father was a public speaker and said that when he gave a speech, people would come up to him and say "Tom, Tom – you were great!" Dad would say "Yeah? What did I talk about?"

"Don't know", was the answer, "But you sure sounded good!"

Mother was the quiet fire of that duo, but there was nothing quiet about my father and there is nothing quiet about any of his kids. My genes are a mixture of sound and

fire, though sometimes
that sound has a
bluster and the fire has
an edge of fury.

⚡⚡⚡

Academics aside,
there was a lot going on
in college. My rock 'n
roll heroes, a group
called The Byrds, were
performing at
Brockport and I heard

that ALL bands were interviewed by the school radio station. Determination kicked in: I WOULD be the one to conduct that interview. The first hurdle was to join the radio staff.

It was the mid-1970s and all the nerdy young men who worked

there thought it was
adorable that a little
blond hippy girl wanted
to join them. Taking me
under their wing, I
wound up interviewing
Roger McGuinn, leader
of The Byrds. Asking
him how it feels to be
out there before a
crowd that absolutely
worships him, his

rambling answer told me that "This guy is stoned to the bone! How is he able to play guitar and sing? How is he even able to stand up?"

There was something familiar about the idea that if you want something badly (in this case performing in a rock band despite being somewhat impaired by marijuana and wine) you somehow charge through.

)()()(

We'd ride around on bikes for hours. One night, I must have hit a stone and flew straight up in the air, flipped

and crashed straight
down on my head.
Luckily, I was with
friends and we walked
the rest of the way
home.

It was summer and
most of the students
were gone but I'd
decided to stay and
work for the school TV
Center -- my radio

buddies told me about that opportunity.

In the main office the next morning, I sat on the sofa telling the receptionist what had happened on the bike ride. After about five words, I slumped over and passed out. The emergency room's verdict was that I'd

had a concussion –
there was nothing to do
but remain still and
rest.

• • •

Let me tell you
about my dog Buck. Like
so many other un-
thought through college
pets, he was a mistake.
Buck lived with me and
three other young

women in a townhouse complex called Brock Manor. Some crazy person rented these lovely homes to students, most of whom had dogs. There were always roving bands of dogs with red or blue bandannas around their necks marching across the parking lot at night

as we'd ride in on bikes
outfitted with battery
operated Wonder-
Lights.

Circumstances
changed and I became
Buck's sole master. I
was moving to an
apartment in town,
above a pottery store.
The big dog had lived
all his life in a large

space with plenty of room to run. Thinking that this move wasn't fair to him, I planned to give Buck to a fellow student who had two little girls, lived in the countryside, and had just lost a dog. The kids would be thrilled and Buck could run free.

We all met at a professor's home to rehearse a play and I'd brought Buck. My friend would leave with him. But Buck must have caught my scent when we were all leaving and the jig was up - I still hear the poor animal's screams.

≈ ≈ ≈

Graduating in 1975 with no idea what to do with my life, I jumped at the chance to take a ride with a friend for her out of town interview. "And you should talk with them, too", she said. "But Amy, isn't this a social work place?" I protested. "Well", she said, "They have an audio visual department and you were always doing that type of stuff in school..."

Her words hit me like a blast from a blunderbuss: I could parlay my school work-study into an actual paying job! Scouring the employment sections (that interview trip, by the way, didn't work out for either of us) I saw a banner ad for "Clerical Opportunities At ABC-TV"

The big ad said that interviews would be held at an Open House in their New York headquarters on 6th Ave. It was the summer of 1975 and I was a 22 year old bundle of insecurity who felt that even with a college degree, I had very little to offer. But I took the bus to the subway from my parents' house in Yonkers and walked straight into the CBS building, also on 6th Ave.

"No dear", said the receptionist, "You want the building up the street." Not a good start.

From a lobby teeming with people who'd seen the same big ad, I was herded to the 20th floor to be interviewed. A similar scene: people sprawled across the floor using each others backs as boards to fill out applications. It seemed hopeless.

Eventually, I was seen by a prim woman who may have been wearing pearls. With my resume and letter of recommendation from a professor in front of her, she said "I see you're a college graduate. These are clerical positions. You can't expect to step into someone else's job..." My words snapped back with a touch of outrage, "I'd never intentionally do that ...".

It all seemed such a waste of time: I had no work qualifications and there were so many people in the halls outside. So I went for broke. "Whose idea was this anyway? How many jobs could there be, clerical or not, 30? 50? Why are you messing with all those young

minds out there?"

When I think back

on this scene, I hear an

out of line college kid

from the suburbs, and

wonder that Ms.

Maleska didn't ask me

to leave. Instead she

said "There's someone

uptown in the news

department who you

should see. His name is Robert Siegenthaler and I'll forward your papers to him".

She did and he called. I was hired as a unit secretary. You can't get any lower on the table of organization, but that didn't matter to me. All the producers in the unit had to meet me and when I walked into Jeff Gralnick's office, almost giddy with the thought that I actually landed this job, he looked up from my papers and asked, "Do you take steno?"

I completely deflated but didn't skip a beat in replying "No, and I don't intend to learn." "Well", Jeff replied, "I guess it's not really all that important. Welcome aboard." He shook my hand: I had a direction and a job!

∞∞∞

Linked to this young producer who was

very good at his job but

very bad with people,

my star rose with his.

Now, he could carry on

with the business of

putting television

broadcasts together

and leave behind all the

people stuff. From the

start, I felt like a big

shot: though the

Senators were

returning HIS calls, I
answered the phone.
For a while, that was
good enough for me.

Soon enough, I
discovered that my
Catholic school outfits,
the cream colored linen
skirts and jackets with
the coordinated
blouses, were not at all
the required, or even

desired, mode of dress here. In fact, this was not only the land of TV news, but TV NETWORK News: after hearing that I'd been hired, my father asked if the position was at the local station or the network. Not aware of a difference, I replied "What?" But there's a big difference. The prevailing sense at the network level, no matter what the job, was that we were "other"; not necessarily better, than local news gatherers. Local news rooms were but planets. Network news was the center of the solar system. In August,

1975, my life had begun

on the sun.

~~

In some ways,

working in TV News was

the ideal job for me.

Everything and

everyone around me was

ultra-cool and that

seemed to be what I

craved. If demeanor

gave away your absolute

awe at either being involved in the coverage of world events or the presence of world shakers, you usually didn't last long. From day 1, I was plenty star struck, but I never let on. My father had always told us kids to "dazzle them with b.s.".

Here are some highlights from those turbulent times:

THE HEADLESS CHICKEN SYNDROME

For years, the larger TV networks had been sitting with the President for an "informal chat" during

the Christmas season.
Equipment was pooled
and my boss was
coordinator. He took
me to DC for a planning
session with a White
House Special
Assistant to President
Jimmy Carter and 4 top
television news
producers, all of them
men. My inner

excitement level was

off the charts!

Out of town jaunts

were considered

excuses for hanky-

panky and since this

was the first time

anyone brought a

secretary to one of

these meetings, it was

probably a foregone

conclusion that we were

conoodling: boss Jeff Gralnick was very handsome, I was all duded up, why not? But I didn't think like that and he didn't either.

But I did ask myself WHAT AM I HERE FOR? Don't get me wrong: I was thrilled to be there! I didn't hear any more after the words *YOU ARE FLYING TO WASHINGTON* …. and couldn't wipe the pride off my face for days (privately because it wasn't acceptable to show animated enthusiasm).

So I stood in my new brown suede suit with the sheep skin

collar surrounded by men who wore casual cool, one of whom was my drop dead handsome supervisor. But he was not a good looking power house to me: he was Jeff, my boss.

We got down to business: who asks the first question? Someone produced a baseball cap and Jeff told me to fill it with numbers. "Make them all ones", he growled under his breath. It was early, there wasn't time to stop for coffee; I made them all ones.

With a slight smirk, the CBS producer announced "I

have #1". The NBC producer said "But I have #1!" Then "But I..." They all looked at me. I turned to the boss and exclaimed "But you told me to make them all ones!"

Of course someone snidely asked "Do you do EVERYTHING he asks?" and then the

room exploded with
laughter.

**Next stop:
the White House!**

Standing in a
White House hallway
lined with 100
poinsettias, most of
them red, that earlier
question hit me again:
Why Am I Here? Even

then, it sounded like a complaint, but it was more confusion than anything else. Jeff had gone into the Red Room, where the interview would be held.

As I stood in the hall, admiring the beauty of this building, a feeling that I should look left came over me.

Jimmy Carter walked past me, nodding a greeting and continued to the session setting. I also nodded and said "How ya doin" to the President, trying hard to disguise my excitement.

The LOOK LEFT sense hit me again. This time it was Roslyn

Carter, heading straight for me, speaking in rapid fire, as if picking up our earlier chat.

"Don't you think he looks so much younger with his hair cut?" she drawled.

Completely dumbfounded by this moment, but focusing

on the "no awe, no emotion at all" mantra, I lied: "Well, I never thought he looked too old to begin with."

She continued, changing topics, as if satisfied she could confide in me, and said "I got so much packin' to do. Don't know how I'm gonna' get it done in time." [They were leaving Monday for overseas meetings. This was Friday.]

In my head, I thought *"there must be any number of staff that can assist these people"*, but I said something completely different: "You know, I think you should relax.

It'll get done. Have a drink or a cup of tea, whatever calms you down. Just do a little at a time and ask someone to give you a hand."

At this point, the President returned. "OK, dear", he said, putting his hand on her shoulder. "Let's go."

Roslyn replied "But we're talkin' here!"

"Hey", I smiled, "Don't want to hold you up. Remember, you got packin' to do!"

They drifted away, into the inner zone of the White House. My boss spoke softly behind me and I could hear the grin in his voice, "Enjoy your chat?"

www

But the job wasn't all fun and trips out of town. It was also exhausting: I felt a constant need to appear interested and busy. The work was loaded with deadlines and pressure. But the worst part for me was believing I was forever playing a role, always feeling the need to appear a certain way. That need has never left me. I'm talking about an attitude or demeanor: something less tangible than clothes or weight.

Something more close
to the bone.

━━

I even interviewed
for another job at ABC
News, in radio. The
radio man asked if I
had lost my mind: his
words were something
like "If you're
considering leaving
because you're bored,

don't come here." The TV man who originally hired me said that if I wanted to look elsewhere, it was my choice to do so. "But if you stay, and I hope you will", he said, "You'll look back on these slow periods with longing. The way this unit works, there's nothing and then there's

everything."

So I stayed.

Many producers

went out for long liquid

lunches until the

proverbial plane fell out

of the sky. Then they

worked like a S.W.A.T.

team. It brought back

memories of my college

interview with a very
stoned rock 'n roller
who was so determined
to play his music, he
defied all obstacles. It
also reminded me of my
father, so outside
himself when speaking
publicly: How were
these people able to
perform? Did they
become someone else at

those moments? *Was
that happening to me?*

Meanwhile, I'd
deposit the producers'
paychecks at the bank
around the corner – no
direct deposit yet - and
marvel at the money
they were paid. On the
other hand, my
paycheck was $129 a
week. Now, there were

dollar signs as well as
stars in my eyes.

⅃ ⅃ ⅃

The first
broadcast I worked was
in November, 1975.
President Ford was in
China and video was
being sent into NY via
satellite, relatively new
technology then. The
pictures came in at

4a.m. and I was
assigned to take notes.

Staying at a
friend's apartment in
New York, all I could
think about was that at
the end of this
program, my 22 year
old name would be in
lights on the screen - I
felt so important, so
"cool"!

The "look interested and alert" mantra took over that early morning. Furiously writing reams of notes I'd never be able to decipher later, using the lingo of the industry to describe different camera shots, I was panicked. I felt like Lucy with the

cherries on the
conveyor belt, the
relentless video kept
coming! In a better
world, someone would
have taken me aside
and said "Look, kid.
What you're doing here
is making a rough
record of what's on
these tapes. The
details of the camera

moves will be filled in later. Think ROUGH".

But of course, no one said this.

The early start to the day and the very long hours may have been part of why I felt important: so much to do and only Mary Jo McKeon could do it!.

After the dawn
satellite, there were
non-stop line up re-
types: White-Out only
works so long.

There was a lot of
waiting around for
information: the on-air
personnel were in China
and instant
communication wasn't
yet possible. Given the

tremendous amount of coordination that goes into even a short broadcast, I'd be at work until midnight (our special program would air in the 11:30pm time slot, delaying the start of the Late Night movie) so "Look Interested and Look

Alert" all day and all night!

About 9pm, we'd head to the studio. This one block walk both thrilled and made me feel self conscious, like maybe I shouldn't be there. But I shoved the negatives inside and strode with purpose.

My assigned location was the videotape room, a dark, cavernous cubicle similar to where the morning satellite was recorded. There were different people at the controls of these machines. They all wore "Look Interested and Alert" faces.

At 11:55, the broadcast was winding down and I slipped into an empty adjoining cubicle to watch my first on-air credit. That's really all I cared about: my name racing by at 90 miles an hour. And I felt the same thrill down my spine

every time my credit
rolled for the next 20
years.

My voice changes
when I talk about my
work in TV – do you
hear it? Or is it just
something I alone
sense? It sounds less
authentic, less real. My
husband says this is

normal because I'm reaching back, trying to describe my feelings then while keeping it interesting now.

Whether it's natural or not, I don't like it. It sounds like 20 years of self-deception.

===

Maybe it's more than my voice. Perhaps, like the S.W.A.T. team producers, the stoned rocker, or my father, I became someone outside myself when I worked. No wonder I was having bouts of confusion. Sometimes I think those moments are still with me.

°°°

So many unique
experiences in my 20+
years at ABC News:
walking on the roof of
the Capitol looking for
camera positions for
coverage of Reagan's
first inauguration,
Buckingham Palace
remote producer for
the wedding of Charles

and Dianna, assisting in the coverage of the White House welcome ceremony for the freed American hostages.

But my favorite assignment was film researcher, sifting through pictures of history, stepping into the 1917 Russian revolution or listening to a King's abdication in 1936.

These jobs usually were given to inexperienced young'uns because it was thought the task didn't call for much more than following a shopping list: find pictures of a specific revolution or a king of England giving

up his throne.

The very early

stuff was usually

motion picture:

crumbling, highly

flammable nitrate film

housed in cool but also

crumbling buildings in

Long Island City.

Dressed in dusty jeans,

I'd sit in the shadow of

a huge billboard for Silvercup Bread while the Hearst chief archivist would clean the old film as it ran through his white gloved fingers. We'd search for the scenes on my laundry list. This man didn't like most of the young'uns who came to see him, probably because they were

usually bored and brash

and thought they knew

everything that

mattered. But he liked

me probably because I

was genuinely

fascinated.

Film that was

stored at ABC News

was not carefully

handled, in fact it was usually so tangled that trying to unravel it would cause it to snap. So when a producer needed video from the Senate Watergate Hearings, specifically Howard Baker asking his famous question "What did the President know and when did he know it?", I was sent to go find it at one of the archives. Quite often, the solution to problems in this era of TV news was to throw money at it.

As a high school kid, I watched the Hearings with the sound turned off and wasn't aware that this question had been asked over and over. My assignment, I thought, was to find a needle in an electronic haystack. The job today would be SO much easier with the Internet - but then the delight of discovery would be SO less thrilling.

Off I went to shop, this time to one of those architectural gems that reek of history and story. Most offices inside the Film Center on New York's 9th Ave. had something to do with the television, film, or music worlds.

After searching
for a couple hours, I
found it! With a smug
smile, I pushed the
"down" button.

The rock band
Kiss, in full white face
makeup-the guys known
for slithering tongues-
was on that elevator.

Entering, I turned to the front and laughed inside my head at the absurdity of this scene: there was a Watergate tape under my arm! I went to the street and hailed a cab back to the office. All in a days work, but what a day for a young'un! Talk about cool!

^^^

Screaming down
the Belt Parkway in
Queens, I tried to get a
fix on the driver. He
was the cameraman
everyone told me was
the best at ABC News.
"It's just a political
filler spot", I said to
myself. "We're not

covering an assassination attempt for God's sake!"

Bob would drive everywhere with both his camera and a police scanner on the front seat. My colleagues thought this was a sign of his devotion to the job. I found it excessive and scary.

In 1980, the
Democratic Convention
was held in Madison
Square Garden and the
television networks
rolled their remote
trucks up the elephant
elevators. After 5
years at ABC, I was
starting to feel part of
the team. My

secretarial status
didn't exactly match
the image I'd created
for myself, but at least
my unit was the elite of
the news division.
Other departments
hated to see us
descend and take over
when there was a big
breaking story, and I
took pride in that.

Occasionally my boss would throw me a bone, that's how I saw it then. Now I think those were bones of creativity that others would've handled from a more jaded perspective. Because I was fresh, there would be less cynicism in my work.

My assignment was to produce a one-minute spot, wrapping up the highlights of the political race. In the time critical world of TV, one minute meant 60 seconds: no more, maybe less but not by much. The pictures I chose would tell the story, there would be no correspondent's voice. But no one said there couldn't be music.

Ray Charles' recording of "New York's My Home (Keep Your California") was my selection. Playing it on a turntable for hours, I continually lifted the needle until there was a sensible 1 minute version on the tape recorder. The music was set, now all we needed were the pictures! That's where Cameraman Bob came in.

Stories circled around Bob, about his boldness - bordering - on - recklessness in the chase for the perfect shot. These tales were told with awe, emphasizing his pursuit of the most original visual angle. Blindly taking the extra mile and a half was not only applauded in this business, it was expected.

A serial killer nick-
named the Son of Sam
held New York City in a
fear grip in the late
'70s and during our
getting-to-know each
other talk in the van,
Bob said he arrived at
the madman's final
attack before the cops
got there. "One of the
victims was trying to

scramble up a fence
with one hand, he said,
"while cupping his
falling eyeball in the
other! I didn't know
what to do: Should I
grab my camera or run
to help the kid?"

Scrunched against
the far side of the
racing vehicle, I yelled,
"You need to tell me

right now what you did."
He said he helped the
boy. "That was the
right answer," I said.
"Now slow the fuck
down." (We swore often
and large in TV news.
Part of the uniform.)

He was impressed
that I'd "edited" the
music and brought it

for us to listen. Any success I had at ABC News and beyond is due largely to people sensing they are included in whatever I try to accomplidh. Very early in my life, I learned that my own reaction might control the outcome. In other words, by showing

someone enthusiasm or
a willingness to work,
that person may be
willing to work with me.
My mother suggested
that "technique" years
earler when I was so
worried about my
father's reaction to the
cost of a blue wool
cape.

()()()

Symbolism and appearances. They are everywhere. Part of the fabric of life. Especially in politics and in television.

Some say Jimmy Carter lost the 1980 election to Ronald Reagan because of the prolonged captivity of the American hostages.

WAIT A MINUTE.
HERE I GO AGAIN,
SPEAKING FROM MY
HEAD AND NOT MY
GUT!!! I CAN HEAR IT,
ALMOST TASTE IT.
ANYONE HAVE A
LADDER I CAN USE
TO STEP DOWN FROM
THIS RARIFIED HIGH
GROUND? I HEAR MY

FATHER'S VOICE,
NOT MINE!

But the
appearances part can
stay and also the
"Especially in ...
television." It does
sound preachy, but it's
true. And in a memoir,
you're supposed to
write what you know.

Carter did lose in 1980 and we broadcast Ronald Reagan's inauguration. It was the first big news event covered by Roone Arledge, the creator of the hugely successful ABC Monday Night Football. He'd been

named president of
both News and Sports.

Our unit flew home
to NY after the
inauguration but
returned a few days
later for a White
House welcome
ceremony honoring the
freed American
hostages. Our location
was a high scaffold on

the South Lawn of the White House. The correspondent was, well, let's call him Mr. ABC News. His producer on the scaffold would be me. Me! To say there were butterflies in my stomach would be a big understatement, but of course I kept that feeling hidden.

Remember the TV rule? Look interested and alert and I'll add "don't show emotion". This reporter was legend within ABC News and had a reputation for extreme impatience. The very idea that I would be involved in anything he did both

thrilled and scared me
silly.

If the cameraman
with all his gear could
climb the scaffold, how
could I complain about a
fear of heights? Soon,
Mr. News arrived out of
nowhere, in his usual
tizzy, ignoring me but
barking about things he

needed and things he shouldn't have to do.

Softly, it began to sprinkle.

Through my walkie-talkie, I asked the executive producer on the ground where I could find an umbrella for the on air and was told "You have to find one yourself"; a panic mixed with tension in the answer, "I've got problems of my own".

Quietly, I descended the steep stairs. Did I mention that I'm petrified of heights? But a producer's job, I said to myself repeatedly, is to protect the "talent"

at all costs. This was
my duty!

An ABC Sports
vehicle was our remote
truck and I found an
umbrella tucked way in
the back. Shutting my
eyes, I climbed back up
the scaffold. Proudly, I
made the presentation,
ready for a compliment
or at least a thank you.

Instead, he looked at the large red and white striped sports umbrella and howled "Young lady, if I use this I will look like a fucking candy cane."

Instantly angry because I'd just cheated death for this? Though he did have a point, I said "With all due respect, sir, you will look like a fucking candy cane or you will get wet."

@@

This was the big time! Who cares if it was by default. I was the Buckingham Palace remote producer for the Wedding of the

Century, England's
Charles and Diana.
Standing on a podium
outside Buckingham
palace, wearing a
headset, in the thick of
ABC News' coverage of
a Royal Wedding, I was
absolutely ecstatic and
felt my life couldn't get
any better. Mixed in
with my pride was a bit

of a self-conscious
feeling but I kept that
as far inside as
possible. The way I felt
that day made me
forget the night
before.

Almost.

Being there on
that podium was the
result of an f-u

argument between two men, one was the originally assigned Palace producer, the other the coordinator of all the remote locations involved in the coverage. A mad scramble to find a replacement resulted in my being assigned.

I had been sent to London as a "filler cutter": my job was to put together stories on things like *"THE GREAT CASTLES OF THE ROYAL FAMILY"* or *"WHO REALLY IS LADY DIANA SPENCER"* – spots to be used to fill time during the multiple hours we'd be on the air.

I stayed in a fancy London hotel but my days were so long that all I could do was stumble into the super-plush bathrobe, order room service, and fall asleep to the in-room movie.

Three nights
before the wedding,
the room phone rang.
One of the arguing duo,
the man who was the
remote coordinator,
literally SCREAMED at
me for not being "at
your assigned station
for the run through".
Having no idea what he
meant, but panicked

with certainty that whatever was wrong MUST be my fault, I stammered that "I had no idea ... was in a dark room all day cutting fillers".

He responded that it was MY job to find out what MY assignment was and he blasted "your unprofessional

behavior". Feeling about

2 inches tall, heart in

my stomach, I

whimpered an apology.

Calling the other

guy, I discovered that

HE had covered at the

dress rehearsal. There

was no need for the call

to my room in the first

place, no need to make

me feel like small, dusty dirt. The remote coordinator was probably covering his behind because HE didn't notify ME. But the guilt I felt at having exhibited "unprofessional behavior" stayed with me for years, far longer than just that

otherwise glorious trip.

Two days later,
the "anchor tigers"
landed (these were
Peter Jennings, Barbara
Walters, other
luminaries) and a huge
coordinating meeting
was held, chaired by
the very tall executive

producer, the man who had first hired me. At one point, someone asked "How many cameras will follow the carriage from the church to the palace? Surely you can't cover the entire Mall!" The big man, who usually wore a very serious demeanor, responded

"There will be 17 stationary and 12 hand-held cameras and don't call me Shirley."

The fancy hotel where many of us stayed played the movie *Airplane* every night, all night. But his reference to the script line from the movie went right over the heads of those

in the room NOT
staying in that
particular hotel.
Instantly, Bob
Siegenthaler became
my hero: to act so cool
under pressure was to
me beyond impressive.
It was my goal.

(((

From London, I
returned to my New

York office, also sarcastically referred to as The Heartbeat of America. The building was so old and out of date, even the phones were the rotary dial type.

We were preparing to cover the landing of Space Shuttle #3, originally scheduled to set down in California.

The coverage would be

handled completely with

personnel from our LA

bureau. But because of

heavy rains, things were

moved to another

landing site, a

government base in

New Mexico, and touch

down was delayed a day

or two.

You might imagine the mad scrambling a late change like this would cause, for NASA and also for the media covering the landing.

It was decided that I would "produce" the Los Angeles correspondent remotely - from a tape room in New York. The reporter would wear a headset for communication with the New York control room, but I didn't dare question what my role was supposed to be.

Internally, though, I grumbled that "the cheap bastards wouldn't even fly me to the West Coast". But there was some type of job to be done, so once again I pushed my reaction down deep inside. However, as I tried to dial the LA office, transferring my coffee to my left hand so I could place the call with my right, the dial wouldn't rotate.

The dial wouldn't rotate.

Thinking this was strange but focused on my assignment; I switched the coffee and used the left hand. Success. The correspondent and I began to chat about covering the landing when the cup of coffee in my right hand slipped through my fingers and the hot liquid splashed onto my blue jeans. "Sorry, Ken. I have a problem here and gotta go. Call you back."

Phoning my NY neurologist, he said "Relax. I'm sure it's nothing. But if you're concerned, go get a cat scan." He made the appointment and results would probably be available the next day.

No call came in from the doctor so I called him. He said "Yes, there's something there. Come in tomorrow and we'll discuss it." Dumbfounded, I said "WHAT? I'll be a wreck by tomorrow. You can't do this!" "I can and I just did" was his answer. "Until tomorrow."

Stunned, I wondered if the snow starting to fall would prevent my father and I even getting to his office.

If there was no trouble in paradise, I would have gone to the doctor's office with my husband. But my love life was a shambles. I was 27 and married to a dashing Brazilian waiter with whom I had very little in common. Having returned to my parents' house, I was starting divorce proceedings. He wasn't a bad guy, really - didn't beat me up or anything – we just lived in different worlds. He was gorgeous and charming and asked me to marry him at a Christmas party with all his Brazilian family and friends in New York. At that moment, I felt that even though we had never discussed this marriage step, to not accept on the spot would deeply deflate his volatile ego. So, I said "Of course". It was a bad plan from the start. The marriage did last 3 years however, but when it was time to

visit the neurologist, I
went with my father.

Despite the snow,
we made it. The scan
was up on a light box.
The doctor pointed to a
mass at the base of my
brain and said "See
that? It has to come
out and it has to come
out now." After 16

years, the shunt inserted in 1966 to bypass the growth in the back of my brain had fallen. The original problem had come roaring back.

Now in complete shock, I asked what would happen if it wasn't removed. Dr. P.

answered "It will grow until it overtakes your head".

"This cannot be happening to me", I thought. "It's something that happens in the movies, maybe, but not to ME."

Thoughts jumbled through my head crazily. A job had been

offered to me and I was seriously thinking of taking it. "Don't do that now", the doc said. "Hold onto your current health insurance for now. The neurosurgeon I work with is here today, across the hall. You and your father should wait outside and

I will ask him to see you."

After one of the longest 10 minutes in my memory, a Dr. S. finally ushered us, two traumatized robots, down a narrow hallway to a small, dark closet of an office. He'd read through my file, he said. Despite my inner fog, I remember thinking that he must be a speed reader because he had gone through it so fast.

"I've just completed a study at Columbia on brain rocks. If you can live with the knowledge that you have a rock in your head, you'll die

someday, but it won't

be from this."

My words were

shaky: "Lord knows I

want to believe you. But

what explains my lack

of strength, my bad

balance? What explains

my headaches?"

He got defensive,

looked actually angry in

his long, white coat and said curtly "I don't care what you believe. I am telling you there is nothing wrong! Now get out there and live your life!"

Almost catatonic now, I opened the door and the first doctor, the neurologist, stood at the end of the hallway. "When do you go in?" he asked in his businesslike but almost cheery voice. The surgeon was behind me, so I was now sandwiched between two massive medical egos. My father, usually the picture of stability not without his own ego, was probably bringing up the rear like he had stones in his shoes. I never asked him about that day.

Starting to answer, the second doctor took over "Yes, I told her she has a brain rock and that there is no need for surgery." The neurologist waved my father and me into his office and shut the door. "I am attendin a three day conference with many of the doctors here at New York Hospital. Dr. S. is one of them. If he hasn't changed his mind by the time we return, we will get another opinion. Your issue needs to be addressed."

The ride home is a blur but I bet there wasn't much chatting.

===

The job offer I'd mentioned to the doctor was very much in the works. My official start date was May 3,

1982. I was on the operating table on that exact date for the removal of a cerebellar astrocytoma and a Torkildsen shunt. I thought my life was over, done. Though it wasn't, it was one hell of a turning point.

&&&

Much of the time following my surgery is so relentlessly horrible that even though it was years ago, I still need to focus on the good memories. And yes, there were some silver linings.

The first gleaming moment concerns my

mother. Immediately before taking ill; and I went from 90 to 0.3 miles per hour in what seems like two days; my mother took me out to look for an apartment of my own.

My marriage was busted. Living with my parents was getting harder every day, for all of us. Probably a week after finding a place, I went into the hospital. The final divorce papers were delivered to my bedside!

I'd go back to my parents' house to recuperate but mother refused to let the rent lapse and not just because of a signed lease. She wanted me to BELIEVE I would one day soon be independent enough to live on my own. It still brings tears, such heart felt encouragement. As I said earlier, my mother's love was bold

and determined and as
deep as the ocean.

~~~

Here's another
shining memory:

It seemed that
every day, flowers were
delivered from the man
who originally hired me.
A florist van would
screech to a stop
outside my parents'

house. The driver knew
us by this time and
would leave the
arrangement or plant
(usually something lively
and multicolored) on
the front stoop. Maybe
it wasn't every day, but
the actual number of
deliveries isn't my
point: I believed some
people cared enough

about me to make an extra effort. I still ask myself why this is so deeply important to me.

***

And this example: I received a phone call from my immediate boss. Because he was so uncomfortable with most people, it was an uneasy miracle for him to actually pick up the telephone, twirl the (rotary) dial and express good wishes. "It's all behind you now", he said. A week later, I was back in the hospital with meningitis. While dealing with this hurdle, I couldn't help but think about how foolish he must feel.

Still, that he made the call touches me to this day.

"

Maybe to fully recover I needed a dose of non-medical bad news. The job I'd been offered was a production position within a new venture between ABC News and

Westinghouse. If the two companies involved had hung in there, maybe it would be in every major market in the world. But they grew weary of hemorrhaging money and CNN was waiting in the wings.

Within days of my surgery, the ABC News people I was scheduled to work with called to say my job was secure and waiting for me to get better, "This is merely a small delay in your start date. Concentrate on regaining strength.

Your job is here waiting for you."

Though it sometimes seemed it would never happen, I did get better and my father and I drove to the SNC facilities in Connecticut 4 or 5 months later. My new bosses were welcoming, upbeat and positive.

"Start whenever you want", they said. I'd begin a month after my visit. ABC was the production side of the venture, Westinghouse the administrative. Despite suggesting my doctor would be happy to reassure someone that I wouldn't fall apart on the job, they said "All we need is for you to come on board".

Weeks passed, a month, then more weeks. No word from them and no return phone calls for a start schedule. Living alone in the apartment my mother kept alive, I was happy to be independent again but deeply depressed with post-illness despair. Nothing could have made me smile.

Despite feeling so low, I was slowly clawing out of a dark place. The last thing I needed was to be ignored. Or maybe it was exactly what I needed: knowing the secretaries would be gone and the bosses would pick up the phone; I crafted a plan and it worked.

"What gives?" I asked in a low dejected growl. "Well", was the reply, "We really need a letter from your doctor for the administrative end of things". He spoke quickly and in a happy tone. "Besides all that, how's it going?" It hit me like thunder and in almost a whisper, I said "Wait a minute, I've got medical bills, rent bills, car bills, no money coming in and you want to know Besides All That, How's It

Going? I think we have nothing more to say to one another."

Putting down the phone, I asked myself what in God's name do I do now?

≫

And here is the best silver lining of that whole sad time: I called the man who first hired me, Bob Siegenthaler... remember him? The person who sent daily flowers, who long ago told me it was my choice to leave but sincerely hoped I'd stay, who'd become my hero in London. "Hello Bob, I don't have a job...". Immediately this

man said "Yes you do.
You start here
tomorrow at 10." No
questions, he didn't skip
a beat.

Years later, I
asked him why he did
that. His answer:
"Because you're one of
our own and we try to
take care of our own."
Flattering words,

perhaps. But troubling nevertheless: was it true? Was I now one of THEM?

%%%

Now almost 30 years old, with all sorts of medical issues, plus the 18 month COBRA clock screaming inside me, I figured my only shot at health benefits

would be a staff
position.

My first attempt
to create a spot for
myself was a brief
reign as The Obit
Queen of ABC News.
Listening to a daily
conference call
discussing the day's
news, I'd note who was
sick. If no name was

mentioned, I'd work on a living notable like the Pope or Bob Hope. But it became a joke after a while, and a waste of money and manpower: if Mary Jo worked on your obit it was a sure bet that you wouldn't kick the bucket.

What was I thinking? How could a New York City bus be the best way to travel when balance was a big problem? Getting back to the office, I raced into a co-worker's office, a crying, humiliated mess.

My colleague had recently returned to

work himself, after a catastrophic illness- he'd had his left cancerous lung removed. He'd be fine, he was told, as long as he followed a certain exercise regimen and quit smoking.

He was walking the wall with his left hand when I came rushing in with tales of buses and lack of balance. "Do you see what I'm doing? What do you want me to do, Mary Jo: feel sorry for you? You have to do what you have to do. Figure out a way to deal with it. A good place to start might be to grab a cab instead of a bus."

My father often used this phrase: "Lucha por la vida (Fight for life)". The words never struck a chord until that afternoon in my friend's office.

♪♪♪♪

The last place in the world I wanted to be was inside a hospital, but this was my assignment. So with a two person camera and lighting crew, and a correspondent, I took off for a New Jersey medical center. The story was a preemie newborn going home after treatment, now a healthy little baby. It was a "feel good" story

and the brass thought
it would be a nice way
to end the week's
newscast.

Just a few days
earlier, the
correspondent had
asked to borrow my
comb to get ready for
her on-camera
appearance. "Only have
a brush", I smiled,

rifling through my bag.
"You're welcome to it
but mind the hairs! At
least they're blond!"
"Yes" the reporter
snapped, "But mine are
real." My smile faded.

Row after row of
newborns no bigger
than the length of an
adult hand, lay on metal
warming plates. They

were so fragile, even
the weight of a baby
blanket could crush
them.

The cameraman
sauntered over to me
and whispered "If we
use the lights, the bulb
could blow." Looking at
these completely
exposed babies, I said
"F... the lights."

Reporter Blondie overheard and chirped "Oh, come on! How often does that happen?" I turned back to the cameraman: "Like I said, Joe, f... the lights." She slinked away.

The story was not only this specific child but the miraculous work conducted at the Hackensack University Medical Center. Shortly after we began taping, pandemonium struck: the electricity briefly shorted. The ward doctor scrambled in mid-interview and maintenance staff flew into the room. The reporter said to me "I hope you're getting this". My response was a curt "You do your job and I'll do mine."

But increasingly, I sensed that this business was more about the chaos one could find in a story than the story itself.

Nothing bad happened in the end:

the power was only momentarily interrupted. The chief building guy did approach me and said "This happened because your lights drained so much juice." TV lights DO pull a huge amount of electricity, but we had decided NOT to

use them. Guess we
made the right call.

Driving back in our
van, the reporter wailed
that she had forgotten
to tape an on-camera
close. She insisted that
we turn around. "No", I
said. "People want to
see pictures of that

beautiful, healthy baby. It's not all about you."

The phone rang in the tape room as I assembled those pictures. "Can we re-assign your crew to cover breaking news." I said "Sure. But what crew?" "They're scheduled to do an on-camera close at The Hackensack Medical Center." Blondie was so determined to get her face on camera, the reporter had made her own arrangements. And guess where she was? Down the street at the hairdresser's!

Finally, the piece had to be approved by

the executive producer before going to air. As we prepared to view it, she told him the on camera close had been nixed by Mary Jo. He never stopped walking to the videotape room but said "When will you learn that you're not always in charge? Mary Jo is the producer and that means SHE's the boss."

My ego felt great! But tangled with a sense of pride was a feeling that the line between issue and image was getting more and more blurred in the minds of more people in this business.

$$$

It was the middle
of 1996, a few days
after the bombing at
the summer Olympics in
Atlanta. It was also the
middle of the night, the
hours when things are
prepared for morning
news programs. I
looked up at an internal
satellite feed from the

ABC News Atlanta bureau and saw the press, not the cops, not the FBI, swarming all over Richard Jewell, a "person of interest". He wasn't charged or even a material witness. The man was leaving his apartment, heading for his car. The images revolted me. "Who in the hell do they think they are?" I asked myself. "Even if he IS guilty, they have no right to stand in judgment. They're ruining this man's life and..."

"Wait a minute, sweetie", said my other voice. "THEY are YOU. If your boss assigns

you to follow Richard
Jewell, what will you
do? Stand with hands
on hips spewing phrases
of righteous
indignation? How far do
you think that will go?
How can you take their
money and trash what
they do? Seems like you
have some decisions to
make."

ΩΩ

"If you were Blue Cross/Blue Shield and I came to you for health insurance, what would you do?" I put this question to a management friend. He answered "I wouldn't touch you with a ten foot pole." "Right", I said. "That's why I need a staff job."

Timing really is everything; within a few weeks, a morning news broadcast was started and I would be a staff videotape producer.

()()

In one of the tape rooms, a red phone hung on the wall. If it rang, it would be a correspondent from the field with a voice track to record. The call would then be transferred to the control room and the reporter spoke live on the air, usually with a picture of his/her face over a map. Meanwhile the tape room worker bees scurried to assemble a story for the next section of the program.

Picking up a telephone and raising the receiver: who even thinks about such a routine motion? No one - until your body won't do it quickly anymore.

I'd race to answer it
with my right hand that
shook so violently, the
hard plastic almost
knocked me cold. If
certain actions,
however, are automatic,
so too become coping
mechanisms and I'd
quick like a bunny
transfer the phone to
my left hand. No one

ever knew there was a problem.

My lack of coordination and strength was due to nerve damage to the area of the brain that controls the right side.

Finding new ways to handle situations is a good thing, but my poor head was being bashed silly in those few seconds switching hands. Yet I never picked up the phone with the left hand: it was an automatic action to lead with my right side. But if ever I managed to knock myself out, at least I had health insurance because I now had a

staff job!

///

Maybe it was a

coincidence, but the

timing was awfully

strange. Just after

sunrise, on the

overnight shift, 4 of us

were handed

interoffice memos.

Each was from a senior

news executive and here's what it said:

"For an important project that I have been asked to complete, please leave me (or fax to me) a <u>short</u> note detailing precisely what you were doing at 4:30 AM EST on Tuesday, January 21. This is not an inquisition. It is part

of an attempt to paint a
worldwide picture of
randomly-selected ABC
News people
performing their duties
at a specific hour of
the day. Please
reply instantly."

None of us fully
appreciated the
significance of 4:30 AM

EST. At the time we received the memo, we were all running around like headless chickens, trying to get things ready in time for air.

4:30 was roughly the time a helicopter crashed carrying 2 ABC News employees and the pilot to their deaths. They had been dispatched under extreme protest to file a report for our program. As often happened, the story they were covering, a Hormel meat packing plant strike, had been hammered into the ground for so long, there was little if anything left. But that

almost never stopped
an executive producer
from insisting that his
or her program be
served. Even if it meant
putting the crew in
danger.

Stories of
coverage gone awry are
complicated and always
terrible, and so many

lives are affected. But I was noticing more and more that the story was the only important thing, even when the story no longer existed. It comes down to a lack of judgment: is there a story here or just pictures? The effect on people's lives seemed to

me to be way down the
priority list.

The interoffice memo
still sits in my drawer.

--__--

A Wall Street
friend hounded me to
call early and tell him
what was going on in
the world. He figured

that since I'd be gathering news from overseas while America slept, he'd get a jump on the day.

"He's just too lazy to get up at 5am", I thought, and never called. Years flew by and now I had a daytime shift. Rumors of a Persian Gulf war had been buzzing for days – it involved a UN deadline for Iraq's withdrawal from Kuwait.

Preparing to meet him at 6:15pm at a bar/restaurant near ABC, I tucked a prepaid phone card (cell phones were not yet widely used) into my blue suede jacket. I was ready to give him the mother of all jumps to his day, even though it would be nighttime, one that would more than make up for all those early morning calls I never made.

We ordered drinks as the bar crowd gathered around the TV

set. "By the way", I said, "The war will begin at 6:30 tonight." He scoffed "How could you possibly know that? I don't believe you". I said "Now isn't this rich? You've been on me for years for inside information and now that I give you

something hot, you say
you don't believe me."

As Peter Jennings
introduced the ABC
News correspondent in
Iraq, red streaks began
to trail across the dark
morning Baghdad sky.
Operation Desert
Storm had begun.

My friend turned to me in astonishment and I handed him my phone card and said, "I think you'll be needing this."

For a long while, the satisfaction of being the coolest person in the room that evening was enough for

me. Over time,
however, doubts crept
in: did a war start on
some kind of TV cue?
Or was this just
another coincidence?

Sunday was a great
day in the NY
newsroom: quiet and
casual, plus there were

no "suits" running around. My job was to help start collecting stories for Monday morning's air.

My colleague in the London newsroom mentioned an odd story from a rural village in western Africa. It involved dead people and livestock and plants

that continued to
thrive - something
about poison gas. The
whole thing struck me
as too unusual to ignore,
but he had no more
details. So I
approached the foreign
news editor on the
other side of the room.
Yes, he knew about it
but said it was nothing -

that only 10 people were dead and "who cares about cows." Despite insisting he knew better, that so often strange sounding stories are either over or under reported, I was dismissed with a "this isn't a big enough story" finality and

returned to my corner
of the newsroom.

By the next
morning's daily briefing,
the number of dead had
risen to 1200 and
arrangements were
being made to send ABC
News people to the tiny
country of Cameroon. A
lake had spewed CO_2

into the air, killing people and cattle but not plants. That same foreign editor and I attended the meeting. He passed a note to me: "How many Cameroonians have to die before it's a news story? Guess the answer is 1200!"

Was this memo meant to be funny? It struck the wrong chord inside me. I was getting increasingly unhappy with the news business, and this cavalier manner almost sent me over the edge. Of course it takes time for a complete understanding of a

report's significance.
But the "it's nothing"
comment was NOT
another way of saying
"let's wait for more
details". It was more a
mocking "only 10 are
dead and who cares
about cows?"

Disgusted as
instances of what I

thought of as uncaring judgment mounted, I decided to quit. Yet every time I made a move to leave, I'd wind up back in some control room. Resolves are only as good as the backbone on which they're made.

ÐÐÐ

Before I knew it, 20 years had gone by, I was 42, my life was this all consuming job that did not resonate at all with my heart. I wasn't married or even dating, there was no room for anything but work.

It seemed foolish to throw away a job that people would kill to have, so I returned to school with the idea of taking an advanced degree. I'd teach a kinder, gentler type of TV news.

Now in a freelance capacity, still working for ABC News, I attended graduate classes on off days (and nights) and loved every minute. It made me think about what I was doing.

My ultimate conclusion was that there is no kinder, gentler type of TV news. After more than 20 years of ambivalent fence sitting I had to leave.

I had to leave

)*((*)

"You fail to realize, Mary Jo, that I am the neurologist of record at ABC's *20/20* for everyone from Barbara Walters on down. What I say goes. This isn't my ego speaking; it's just the way it is."

I was now about 45 years old and the Operations Producer for *20/20*. That any work organization – be it a tv station or a shoe store - would have a neurologist of record was crazy. I'd gone to see my doctor because a nervous breakdown was just around the corner and now I knew everyone else had similar worries.

In tears, I stammered to this man in his long white coat: "How long have you known me to sob over my stupid job?" He answered "Just about as long as I've known you. So how long do you want? A month? A year? The rest of your life?" It took me more than a minute to process what the doctor was talking about: a sick leave salary! Stunned, I muttered "I'll get back to you".

But I just couldn't do it, couldn't continue to take their money. It sounds foolish that I didn't take the deal, even to me at times, especially when trying to balance the checkbook. But after so many years of feeling like a fake, adding

fraud to the list wasn't
an option.

',•',•

What other job
could I apply for?
Television production
was what my résumé
reflected. Since those
paper outlines are
designed to define
where your experience
is, I told myself, get

some other experience.

Go back to school.

~~~

If it seems like
I've spent a lot of time
here, I have. This was a
huge part of my life.
Throughout, my
parents, who were
enormously proud to
introduce me as "our

daughter, the network TV producer", never understood my inner conflict. But my mother could probably tell you every event I worked on and my father glowed when I picked up the bill.

The ABC News days, and the people who were in them, still

influence me. Only a very few are still in my life but most live on in my memory. What a time it was!

≠≠≠

It's true about one door opening when another closes. In the middle of my ABC News days, I asked my father for guidance on how to handle my money. He answered that I could use "...my guy. He's not very aggressive, but he's honest". That was Garry. Took a couple years but we're married now. He is the love and the light of my life.

The door Garry waited behind opened

the moment I left TV because my mind and my heart unlocked that moment. If this sounds a bit too new-age for some, wait! There's more!

Early in our courtship, I consulted a psychic, ostensibly for her opinion about a job offer from good ole'

ABC (her answer: SOUNDS LIKE THE SAME OLD DANCE), but really I was so excited about Garry, I wanted to shout from the mountaintops! She asked where he came from: "He just sort of fell off the pumpkin truck", I said. Loraine the Seer was furious at this response and she actually yelled, wagging her finger at me. "The spirits have been struggling for millennia to bring you two together! I would hope you'd have more respect than to blithely say he just fell off a truck somewhere!"

Garry is an accountant, a numbers guy. Loraine nearly fell off her purple-draped chair when I told her: "He's your weakest link!" Listening to the taped sessions with him, Garry wanted to know who was calling him a weak link; but of course he knew her words meant that HE fulfilled MY weak link.

Maybe this really IS a bit too new age: let's move on to Library School.

ΔΔΔ

"You're gonna WHAT? You have to do somethin' about your hair!" was a friend's reaction to news of my plan to study for a library degree. His bewilderment had to do with Hollywood's portrayal of librarians wearing buns and my curly short hair wouldn't allow that; but not wearing a bun was the least of the obstacles.

The reaction I get when people learn I switched from TV producer to librarian is almost always total confusion. My standard response is that a responsible journalist will research his or her subject before reporting on it, so maybe I should have learned research skills before working in TV news. Guess the key adjective is RESPONSIBLE.

When Garry and I found a wonderful apartment in Rockville Centre on Long Island, I trotted down to the nearby public library

and applied for a job.
The woman who became
my supervisor called
the next day: "You have
a master's and 20 years
experience in TV: the
job I can offer is
shelving books. Do you
want this job?"
My answer was that I'd
really like HER job; I
wanted to be a

reference librarian. But I had no idea how to answer the questions she tackled. Yes, I wanted to immerse myself in a library environment and maybe learn things like which dictionary is best or how to find the selling price of a stock bought twelve years ago.

But you can't grasp
how to conduct
successful research
through osmosis.
Returning to school, I
enrolled in a Library
Science program.

&&&

Going to school
was easy for me;

finding a niche was not.
Maybe as the oldest
student in the room, I
took more interest in
school. But I wanted to
do something that
mattered to me,
something I felt would
make a difference to a
life. Answering
questions about
dictionaries and stocks

is useful to some, but I needed more.

Handing a Turkish speaker a book-on-tape that was read in both Turkish and English, he grinned and asked "How much?" Because English is my only language, I spoke simple words to explain there was no charge; it was a book he

could borrow and
return to the library.
But it puzzled me why
he would assume there
was a fee.

An ESL specialist
told me most of the
world's libraries are
available only to
scholars, and only inside
the building. "That's
wrong", I thought and

my niche was defined.
In the public library
world, as in many
worlds, it's called
outreach.

We moved to the
Capital District of New
York in 2005. I was 52,
and although I thought
my resume was a shoe-
in, finding a job proved

difficult. We'd chosen a spot full of natural beauty but it also had a university that offered a library degree and the competition was fierce. Plus, though there were plenty of tiny, town owned libraries around, they didn't have to hire a card-carrying librarian

if the population served
was below a certain
number. Of course, I
wasn't aware of any of
these things
beforehand. All I knew
was that although I
lived in a beautiful area,
a job wasn't
forthcoming. Finally, a
part time librarian
position in a college

opened and it soon morphed into full time.

Almost everything in academe is driven by the curriculum. Though school taught me there are different types of librarians, I didn't dwell on the details. Consequently, my world changed when I found out an academic library position is not at all like a public library job. Having spent the last bunch of years cultivating diversity, I found myself steering students to information on their papers, due yesterday. Of course, there is satisfaction in guiding young minds, but it just wasn't the same for me.

My job became just that, a job. Despite having made some life-long friends; I once again felt the need to get out.

We'd moved to a quiet rural area and my commute was over 20

miles each way.
Dissatisfied with the
work and the drive, and
with frustration
growing daily, I retired.
It was 2012 and I was
59.

++

Our town has a
senior luncheon a few
days each week.
Sometimes I go, not

just to eat but to engage the group in a short Tai Chi routine. A fellow diner, a WWII vet, heard that I was writing a memoir. He asked "Did you have an interesting life or something?" I answered "Well, yes, I did. And I still do. And so do you."

His words are worth thinking about: what is an "interesting life"? Not necessarily an outstanding life or or even one that's noteworthy. And isn't everyone's view of interesting or noteworthy different? My life continues – there's a completely

different writing
project inside me - but
certainly in the eye of
this beholder, it
continues to be an
interesting journey.
And from the beginning,
an interesting life.

MORESOMEDAY

This work is dedicated to Garry Fischer, Jeff Gralnick, and Sr. Mary Josina: 3 people who never met but have given me gifts beyond measure.

Made in the USA
Middletown, DE
26 October 2020